Contents

Words in **bold** in the text are explained in the glossary on page 44.

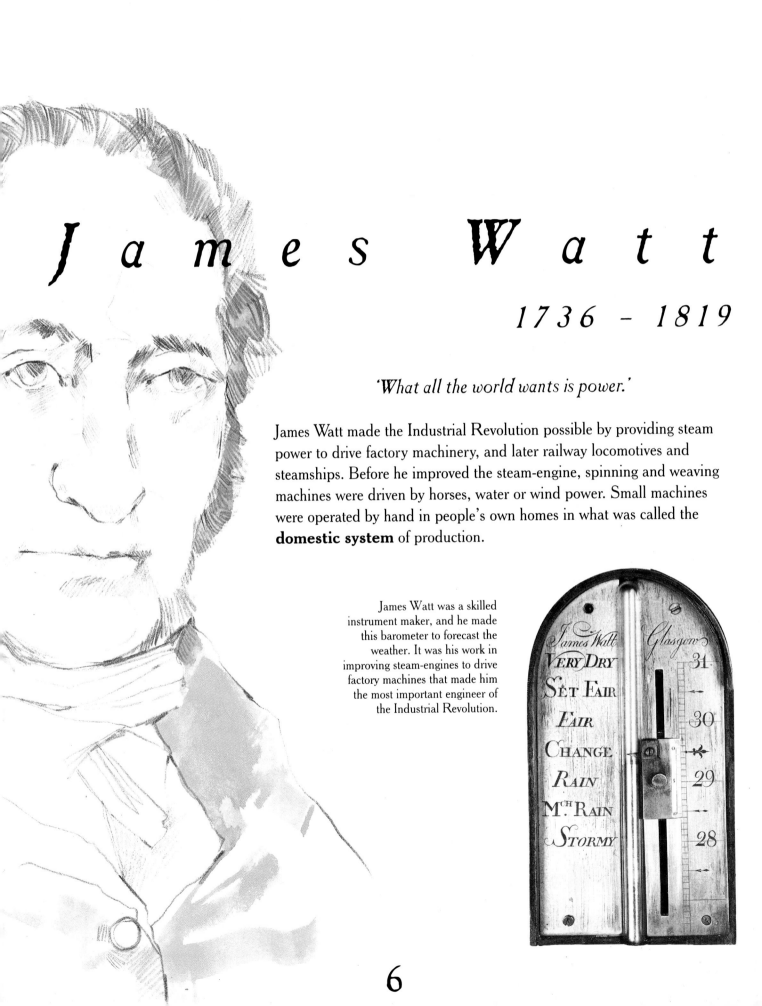

James Watt

1736 – 1819

'What all the world wants is power.'

James Watt made the Industrial Revolution possible by providing steam power to drive factory machinery, and later railway locomotives and steamships. Before he improved the steam-engine, spinning and weaving machines were driven by horses, water or wind power. Small machines were operated by hand in people's own homes in what was called the **domestic system** of production.

James Watt was a skilled instrument maker, and he made this barometer to forecast the weather. It was his work in improving steam-engines to drive factory machines that made him the most important engineer of the Industrial Revolution.

Childhood illnesses kept Watt from attending school. Instead he learnt many useful skills in his father's engineering workshops. At the age of nineteen, he left his home in Scotland and moved to London to train as a scientific instrument maker. In just one year, instead of the usual four or five, he gained the qualification he needed. But his hard work left him exhausted, and he had to return to Scotland.

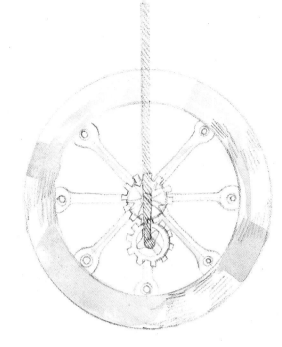

Watt did not invent the steam-engine. Fifty years earlier, Thomas Newcomen built this simple steam-engine to pump water out of tin mines. Watt studied Newcomen's engine and decided that he could build a better one.

Watt went to work for the University of Glasgow, making and repairing various scientific instruments. A short time later, he was asked to repair a working model of a steam-engine used for pumping water and invented by Thomas Newcomen in 1705. It was the opportunity he had been waiting for. When he had finished the repair, he knew that he could build a much better engine.

Over the next few years, Watt built many steam engines. The advantage of his engines was that they not only used only a quarter of the coal needed by earlier engines, so they were much cheaper to run, but they were also more powerful.

DATE CHART

1736
Watt is born at Greenock in Scotland.

1754
Starts training as a scientific instrument maker.

1764
Marries Margaret Miller. Starts work on steam-engines.

1773
Margaret dies during childbirth.

1775
Watt goes into business with Matthew Boulton to manufacture steam-engines.

1776
Marries Ann McGregor.

1782
Builds the first rotary steam-engine to drive factory machinery.

1819
Dies and is buried in Handsworth Church, near Birmingham.

In Watt's steam-engine, a coal fire heated the water to make steam. This steam pushed a piston up, which made the beam at the top rise. As the steam condensed back into water, the beam fell. This up-and-down action could be used to pump water out of mines.

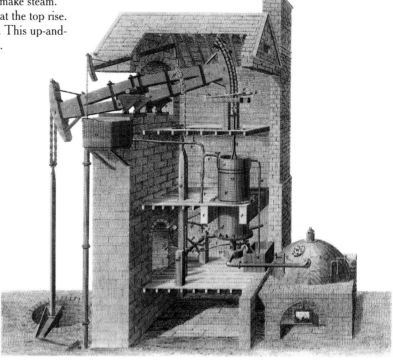

Although Watt was a very successful engineer, he faced other problems. Throughout his life, he suffered a great deal from depression, and worried constantly about his health. While he was working away from home, his wife died while giving birth to their second child.

Watt moved south to Birmingham and went into partnership with Matthew Boulton, building steam-engines that could drive all kinds of machinery. Engines were used to lift coal to the surface in mines and to drive the great hammers used in the iron industry. Richard Arkwright was the first person to use one of Watt's engines to drive machines in a cotton mill, thus starting the factory system. For the first time, mass production in factories was possible, using steam-engines to drive spinning and weaving machines. One enthusiastic writer of the time, a Mr Farey, was in no doubt how important this was:

> 'Seven hundred and fifty people work in a cotton mill, and with the help of the steam-engine they will spin as much thread as 200,000 people could without any machines ... The invention of the steam-engine has changed industry as the invention of gunpowder changed warfare.'

Although James Watt did not actually invent the steam-engine, his improvements were crucial to the success of the Industrial Revolution. Because of him, people no longer had to depend on natural sources of power such as wind or water.

Cotton spinning machines in factories like these in 1835 were driven by steam-engines. These machines could spin hundreds of threads instead of just the one thread on hand-powered spinning wheels. Watt's steam-engines made the factory system possible.

Watt's work made him wealthy and famous. Wherever he went, he and his second wife, Ann, were treated as celebrities. Even after he retired he kept inventing new ideas, and was happiest when he was busy in his attic workshop.

After his death at the age of eighty-three, a statue of Watt was placed in Westminster Abbey. However, the best tribute to his work is that the unit which measures electric power, the watt, is named after him.

Watt's most important improvement used cogs and wheels so that the steam-engine could turn wheels and drive machinery in the new cotton mills and factories. This is called a rotary engine.

OTHER IMPORTANT ENGINEERS

Thomas Newcomen (1663–1729)
– the inventor of an early steam-engine used for pumping water out of coal mines.

Richard Arkwright (1732–92)
– an inventor and businessman who invented a machine, the spinning-frame, that could produce strong cotton thread.

William Murdock (1754–1839)
– the first person to use gas from coal to light homes and offices.

Joseph Montgolfier

1740 – 1810

If man had been intended to fly, God would have provided him with wings.'

So wrote the English poet William Cowper in 1784, the same year that a person flew for the first time in a balloon. For thousands of years, people had dreamed of being able to fly. Joseph Montgolfier and his brother Jacques were the first people to turn that dream into a reality, 120 years before the first aeroplane flight.

Leonardo da Vinci (1452–1519) was an Italian painter, architect and engineer. He was sure that one day people would be able to fly, and he designed this helicopter. But it was nearly 300 years later before anybody actually flew.

The Montgolfier brothers were the sons of a wealthy paper manufacturer who lived in southern France. Both brothers grew up with a keen interest in science. They were always looking for new ways of making paper, as well as new uses for it, so they could increase their sales, but Joseph was the first to think about the possibility of people flying. He began to try all kinds of experiments. First he tried simple parachutes, which he tested by jumping off the factory roof. Then he began to think about an 'air machine' that would be filled with a gas that was lighter than air. An English scientist had recently discovered hydrogen, a gas that is lighter than air. Joseph was eager to find out whether it was possible to lift heavy loads such as people, using hydrogen.

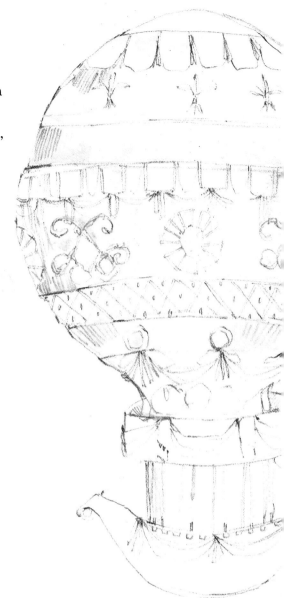

This strange-looking machine, designed in 1811, was supposed to help people to fly like a bird. Many early ideas for flying were quite hopeless and dangerous.

Meanwhile Jacques, who had trained as an architect, became fascinated by Joseph's theories and the two brothers set to work on a series of experiments. They were sure that there was an easier way than using hydrogen to make a balloon rise up. Hydrogen is extremely dangerous because it catches fire very easily.

The Montgolfiers discovered that if they filled a paper bag with smoke it would rise. At first they thought they had discovered an entirely new gas, which they called 'electric smoke'. In fact, as they found out later, it was just hot air, which becomes lighter than normal air as it heats up.

Soon they were ready to show off their discovery. In a field by the River Rhône, they launched a large, globe-shaped balloon filled with hot air from a fire placed under the launching platform. To everyone's amazement, it climbed high into the sky and flew for about half a mile before crashing. No machine had ever flown so high or so far before.

It must have been a very impressive sight when the Montgolfiers' balloon rose into the sky above the Royal Palace of Versailles just outside Paris, France. This eighteenth-century engraving shows the historic flight, on 19 September 1783.

News of this flight caused great excitement throughout France, and Joseph and Jacques were invited to demonstrate their invention in Paris, in front of the king and queen, Louis XVI and Marie-Antoinette. They built a beautifully decorated balloon, but when they tried it out it was destroyed by a sudden storm. They therefore built a new, stronger one, ready for the royal demonstration.

The artist of this picture, drawn in 1794, seems to have imagined a flying village attached to a balloon.

The king thought that balloon travel was far too dangerous for people, so the first air travellers on this splendid occasion were a cockerel, a duck and a sheep. The balloon sailed for over two miles before landing safely. One of those in the large crowd watching was the American scientist and statesman, Benjamin Franklin. Another spectator remarked to him, 'What good is it?', and Franklin replied, 'Of what good is a new-born baby?'

After this success, the king was persuaded to allow a few brave volunteers to risk a journey in the balloon. Even the Montgolfiers were nervous of going up in their own invention. Only Joseph, who took just one trip, flew in the balloon.

Unfortunately, the great upheaval of the **French Revolution** put a stop to further experiments. Joseph returned to the family paper business. But it is as pioneers of the first people-carrying aircraft that Joseph and his brother are remembered, and in France a hot-air balloon is called 'une montgolfière'. As Antoine Rivaral, an observer of the first flight, exclaimed:

'At last we have discovered the secret for which the centuries have sighed: man will now fly – master of the earth, the waters and the air.'

These expensive ivory snuff boxes are decorated with miniature paintings of balloons. One of them shows the first balloon accident. These boxes show that wealthy and important people were very interested in ballooning.

OTHER PIONEERS OF BALLOON FLIGHT

Jean Blanchard (1753–1809) – he flew in the first balloon to cross the English Channel in 1785, but was later killed in a balloon accident.

John Jeffries (1744–1819) – a doctor who accompanied Blanchard on his cross-channel flight.

Jacques Charles (1746–1823) – a physician who made the first ascent in a hydrogen-filled balloon, in 1783.

Thomas Telford

1757 – 1834

'I met ruts that I actually measured as four feet deep and floating in mud. The only mending it receives is the tumbling in of some loose stones which jolt a carriage in the most intolerable manner.'

In the late eighteenth century, the state of most British roads was dreadful, as you can see from these words of Arthur Young, a well-known writer. The government, however, was reluctant to spend much money on improving the roads, so many were improved or built by private companies. Travellers paid to use these 'turnpike roads', as they were called. Engineers were needed to construct smooth road surfaces, along which stagecoaches could travel at speed.

Thomas Telford was one of the most important road engineers of the Industrial Revolution, and nearly all his achievements are still in use today. He started his working life as an **apprentice** stone-mason. But he rose to become a great civil engineer, the '**Colossus** of roads', as one writer of the time, Robert Southey, called him.

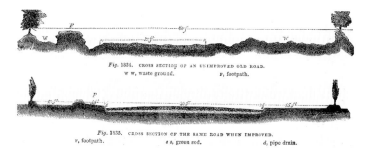

Fig. 1834. CROSS SECTION OF AN UNIMPROVED OLD ROAD.
w w, waste ground.   F, footpath.

Fig. 1835. CROSS SECTION OF THE SAME ROAD WHEN IMPROVED.
v, footpath.   s s, green sod.   d, pipe drain.

The top picture shows a road before it had been improved and the bottom picture shows it with a new, smooth surface.

14

A horseman is paying a toll at the Tyburn Turnpike in London, England.

At first, Telford built homes and prisons, but he was eager to take on larger building projects. After building several bridges, he was finally employed to construct an important canal. It took more than ten years to complete the Ellesmere Canal, which carried raw materials and finished goods from Wales to the River Mersey.

Telford was then made responsible for repairing and building a network of roads in the Scottish Highlands. The problems he faced in building roads in such a mountainous area were enormous. But he overcame these difficulties by inventing a new solid gravel road surface that could take wheeled vehicles and cope with the Scottish weather. He built 1400 km of new roads, and eleven bridges. The success of these roads changed the whole way of life in the Highlands. Villages were no longer so isolated, local people could use carts instead of packhorses to carry goods, and people's cottages were improved because better building materials could be moved.

The Caledonian Ship Canal in Scotland was one of Telford's greatest achievements. There were many engineering difficulties that had to be overcome.

DATE CHART

1757
Telford is born at Glendinning in Scotland.

1793
Begins to work at building canals.

1802
Starts work on the roads in the Scottish Highlands.

1815–26
Builds a new road from London to Holyhead.

1828
Completes the building of St Katherine's Docks in London.

1834
Dies, and is buried in Westminster Abbey.

This map shows Telford's roads in the Scottish Highlands. These new roads were very difficult to build, but they made life much better for the people who lived in these remote areas.

OTHER IMPORTANT ENGINEERS

John Metcalfe (1717–1810) – built many roads across difficult land in the Pennine areas of northern England. Blind from the age of six, he was known as 'Blind Jack'.

John MacAdam (1756–1836) – inventor of the 'macadamizing' system of road-making which uses broken granite to make a strong surface.

Marc Brunel (1769–1849) – fled from the French Revolution to the USA and then to Britain, where he improved the port of Liverpool and built a tunnel under the River Thames.

After this success, Telford was ready for his greatest challenge. The British government wanted to improve the slow and difficult journey between Ireland and London. Ireland was then governed by Britain, and many official travellers used that route. Telford was given the job of building a new road from London to the port of Holyhead in northern Wales, from where a ferry could be taken to Ireland. The main difficulty he faced was making a smooth road through the Welsh mountains. Telford used the knowledge that he had gained from his work in Scotland, using explosives to blast away rock to make new passes for the road.

Telford proudly described his achievement:

'This road, established through a rugged and mountainous district, partly along the slope of rocky precipices, and across inlets of the sea, where the mail and other coaches can now travel at the rate of ten miles an hour, was indeed an arduous undertaking, which occupied fifteen years of incessant exertion.'

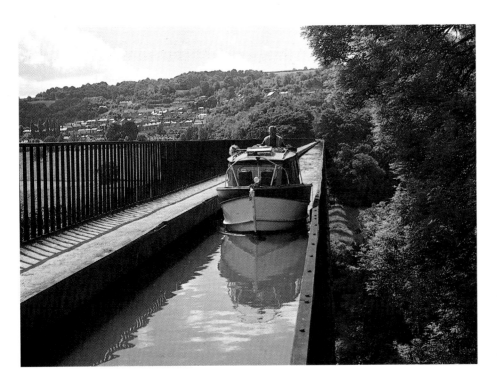

This aqueduct, completed by Telford in 1805, still carries the Ellesmere Canal across the Dee Valley. It has been described as one of the 'wonders of Wales'

Several bridges had to be built. The most famous, the Menai Straits **suspension bridge**, is still used today.

Thomas Telford never married; instead, he devoted himself to his work. When he died, he was buried at Westminster Abbey. His bridges and other work stand as his memorial, but a further recognition of his importance came in 1963, when the new industrial town of Telford in Shropshire, England, was named after him.

The Menai Straits Bridge looks just the same today as it did when Telford built it. It links the island of Anglesey to the rest of Wales.

Mary Wollstonecraft
1759 – 97

How many women waste life away who might have practised as physicians, run a farm or managed a shop?'

Two hundred years ago, women did not have the same rights as men. Very few of them owned property. They were not allowed to vote or to become doctors or lawyers, and were supposed to obey their husbands at all times. Most women as well as men accepted this situation, but a few people were very angry. However, anyone who argued for women's rights was usually made fun of and criticized.

Mary Wollstonecraft was a **feminist** determined to lead an independent life and to help other women do the same. She said:

'I do not wish women to have power over men but power over themselves.'

Wollstonecraft was ahead of her time when she said that women and men should be treated equally. She felt a great deal of frustration and sadness in her life.

18

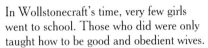

In Wollstonecraft's time, very few girls went to school. Those who did were only taught how to be good and obedient wives.

From an early age, Wollstonecraft was certain that if women had the same education they would be equal to men. She therefore set up a school for girls, but she had very little support for her project. In the end, the school had to close.

Instead, Wollstonecraft turned to writing. These were exciting times in which to write. America had won its independence from Britain, and the French Revolution overthrew the French king, Louis XVI and shattered the power of the wealthy families. Wollstonecraft welcomed these movements towards freedom. Soon afterwards she wrote her most important book, *A Vindication of the Rights of Woman*. She pointed out that many of the new factories of the Industrial Revolution employed women on very low wages, as if they were slaves.

The book caused an uproar. Very few people agreed with her. Another writer, Horace Walpole, called her a 'hyena in petticoats'. Both men and women accused her of trying to stir up trouble.

Wollstonecraft had difficulty finding happiness in her life. Her opinions and her behaviour were frequently criticized. Eventually, when she married William Godwin, another writer, she seemed to have found happiness. However, it did not last long, as she died a few days after giving birth to their daughter Mary, who also became an author, writing the famous book *Frankenstein*.

Nowadays, most people agree that women and men should have exactly the same rights and opportunities. But Wollstonecraft would be angry that, in spite of this, there is still discrimination in many places.

William Wilberforce

1759 – 1833

'The sights I witnessed may I never look on such again – this is a dreadful trade.'

This ship's captain was talking about a trade in human beings – the slave trade. African people were taken against their will from West Africa to the Americas, often on British slave ships. The conditions on them were appalling and many people died. Slave labour was used in the Caribbean islands, part of the **British Empire**, to grow tobacco and sugar. British ship owners, merchants and landowners made huge profits from the trade, which were used in part to finance the Industrial Revolution.

William Wilberforce and some of his friends fought hard to end slavery. Wilberforce became a Member of Parliament when he was only twenty-one years old. At first, people did not expect him to achieve anything important, because he did not seem to care about anything.

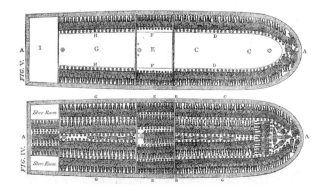

This diagram shows how tightly the slaves were packed below the decks of a slave ship. It was used by those trying to stop the terrible slave trade.

Some white people became very rich by using slaves on their farms and plantations in the Caribbean and the USA. Slaves were frequently beaten and even killed.

OTHER CAMPAIGNERS AGAINST SLAVERY

Granville Sharp (1735–1813) – organized a society to fight slavery in 1787.

Thomas Clarkson (1760–1846) – gathered evidence on the slave trade for anti-slavery books and pamphlets.

Anti-Slavery Society (founded 1823) – the leader of the campaign to end slavery, this organization is still working to end the various kinds of slavery that exist even today in some parts of the world.

DATE CHART

1759
Wilberforce is born in Hull.

1780
At the age of twenty-one he becomes the Member of Parliament for Hull and works closely with William Pitt, the Prime Minister.

1785
He begins campaigning against the slave trade.

1797
Marries Barbara Spooner.

1807
Trading in slaves by British ships is stopped. Wilberforce starts his campaign to end slavery in the British Empire.

1823
Helps to set up the Anti-Slavery Society.

1833
Wilberforce dies just as Parliament agrees that slavery should end.

However, gradually Wilberforce became a strong Christian and a great **humanitarian.** He decided that he should lead the fight in Parliament to stop slavery. Together with some of his friends, nicknamed 'the Saints', he gathered evidence of the horrors on the British slave ships. Descriptions like this one by a slave shocked people and helped Wilberforce's campaign:

'The white people acted in such a savage manner and I had never seen such brutal cruelty. The shrieks of the women and the groans of the dying made it a scene of horror. Two of my countrymen who were chained together, preferring death to a life of misery, jumped into the sea.'

Wilberforce was angry with those Members of Parliament who had become rich as a result of slavery and who voted year after year to keep it. He said: 'I blame no one. We are all guilty of allowing this dreadful evil to go on!'

However, more and more people supported Wilberforce, and finally British ships were stopped from trading in slaves. Then Wilberforce turned to stopping slavery altogether, campaigning hard for over twenty years with the Anti-Slavery Society. Parliament eventually agreed, and all slaves in British lands were given their freedom. The slave owners were paid to make up for the loss of their slaves. William heard this news just three days before he died:

'Thank God, that I should have lived to witness a day in which England is willing to give twenty million pounds for the Abolition of Slavery.'

21

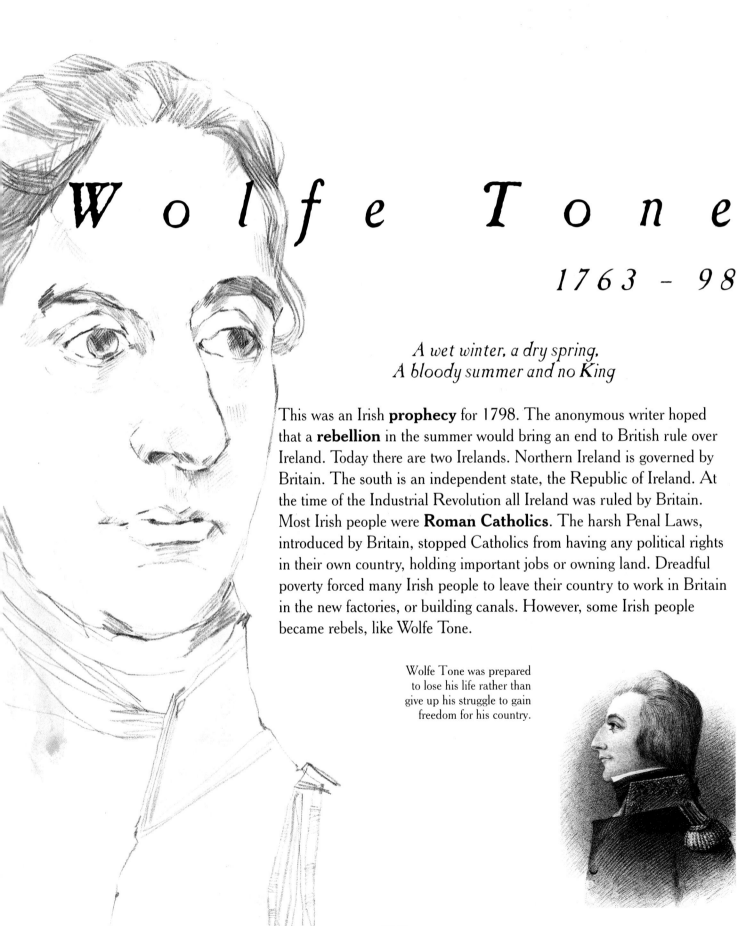

W o l f e   T o n e

1763 - 98

A wet winter, a dry spring,
A bloody summer and no King

This was an Irish **prophecy** for 1798. The anonymous writer hoped that a **rebellion** in the summer would bring an end to British rule over Ireland. Today there are two Irelands. Northern Ireland is governed by Britain. The south is an independent state, the Republic of Ireland. At the time of the Industrial Revolution all Ireland was ruled by Britain. Most Irish people were **Roman Catholics**. The harsh Penal Laws, introduced by Britain, stopped Catholics from having any political rights in their own country, holding important jobs or owning land. Dreadful poverty forced many Irish people to leave their country to work in Britain in the new factories, or building canals. However, some Irish people became rebels, like Wolfe Tone.

Wolfe Tone was prepared to lose his life rather than give up his struggle to gain freedom for his country.

Tone came from a **Protestant** family, so he was able to become a lawyer. He wanted people of all religions to unite against the way Ireland was ruled by Britain. Together with some friends, he set up the Society of United Irishmen. They demanded that everybody should be allowed to vote and that discrimination against Roman Catholics should stop.

Tone was inspired by the French Revolution, with its talk of freedom and belief that everyone is equal. As Britain and France had been at war since 1793, Tone persuaded the French to invade Ireland. Forty-three ships carried nearly 14,000 soldiers to the Irish coast in December 1796, but a terrible storm broke up the fleet before any of the soldiers could be landed. Tone was desperately disappointed, and wrote in his diary:

'We were close enough to throw a biscuit ashore ... but the weather fights against us.'

This picture shows French soldiers being fired at by British soldiers as they landed in Ireland. The British army had many more soldiers than Tone.

Tone fled to France, but he was determined not to give up. Many ordinary Irish people were ready to help him and to fight for their own freedom. When rebellion broke out in different parts of Ireland, Tone returned on a French ship to fight alongside his countrymen. As he sailed into Lough Swilly with just 3,000 troops, he knew the serious risk that he was taking:

'If we are taken, my fate will not be a mild one; the best that I can expect is to be shot.'

DATE CHART

1763
Tone is born in Dublin, Ireland.

1785
Marries Matilda Witherington.

1789
Becomes a lawyer in Dublin.

1791
Helps set up the Society of United Irishmen.

1794
Begins to seek help from France to overthrow British rule.

1795
Visits the USA.

1796
Attempts to invade Ireland with French soldiers, but fails.

1798
After the failure of another rebellion, he is taken prisoner. He commits suicide in Dublin and dies on 19 November.

23

The Irish rebels set up this camp at Vinegar Hill. It became crowded with families trying to get away from British soldiers. There were not enough tents, so people slept out in the open. They brutally executed some Protestants that they had taken prisoner.

The Irish uprising failed and the British took Tone prisoner. Throughout Ireland, people suspected of supporting the rebellion were tortured, beaten and killed. Tone was taken in chains to a trial in Dublin. He spoke with the bravery of a soldier who knew that he was going to die.

'I wish not for mercy. The favourite object of my life has been the independence of my country. I have done my duty.'

Tone saw himself as a soldier who had fought for his country, and he expected to be shot, the usual way that soldiers were executed. But the British hated him, and sentenced him to death by hanging, a slower and more painful death. He refused to allow the British to execute him in that way, and early in the morning of the day he was due to hang, he cut his throat with a small razor knife. For a week he suffered in agony before dying. He was only thirty-five years old.

Many more people died before southern Ireland gained independence. Even then, arguments and violence continued over whether or not the north and south of Ireland should one day be united and independent in the way that Wolfe Tone wanted.

At the battle of Vinegar Hill, the British army attacked the rebel camp and defeated the rebellion for some time, British soldiers continued to search out and kill scattered rebels all over Ireland.

No UNION, Erin go Brach!

The rebels, like this Irish Chief, were brave but badly organized. Tone wanted the Irish people to rise up against British control of Ireland. 'No Union' meant Irish freedom from Britain.

OTHER IRISHMEN WHO FOUGHT FOR INDEPENDENCE

Napper Tandy (1740–1803) – a revolutionary who believed that only violence would bring independence to Ireland.

Daniel O'Connell (1775–1847) – 'The Liberator', who successfully campaigned for equal rights for Roman Catholics, and in 1841 began a campaign for Irish independence.

Robert Emmett (1778–1803) – tried to organize an Irish uprising in 1803, but was hanged after it failed.

Robert Owen

1771 – 1858

'The children are most cruelly beaten with a horsewhip, strap, stick, hammer, handle, file or whatever tool is nearest to hand, or are struck with the clenched fist or kicked.'

This former factory worker's shocking evidence to a government inquiry described the way child factory workers were treated during the Industrial Revolution. Most poor British children at that time did not attend school, but worked for up to seventeen hours a day in dangerous and unhealthy factories for very low wages.

However, some factory owners were shocked at the way in which both children and adult workers were treated. Robert Owen spent his life fighting for improvements to help the poor.

In the early nineteenth century, thousands of young children from poor families worked in cotton mills like this one.

OTHER REFORMERS

Richard Oastler (1789–1861) – an opponent of child labour in factories, which he compared to slavery.

Robert Dale Owen (1801–77) – the son of Owen, who became a member of the US Congress and a leading campaigner for women's rights and an end to slavery.

26

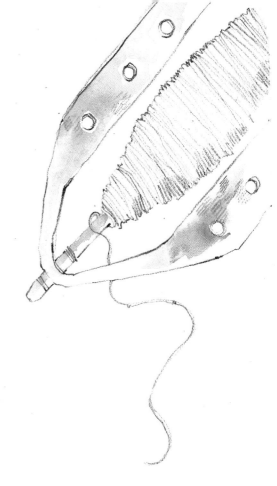

At the age of nine, Owen left school and moved to Manchester, where he worked as a shop assistant. He learnt what it was like to work hard for long hours and low wages, but by the age of nineteen he had risen to be in charge of a cotton mill. He then married Caroline Dale, whose father owned an important spinning mill at New Lanark, Scotland. Soon Owen was manager of the mill.

Owen was determined to prove that he could treat his workers well and still make a profit. He built good houses and set up a cheap shop for them. His most popular act was to reduce the hours they had to work.

Politicians and writers went to see the factory. Owen told them:

'It does not appear to me necessary for children to be employed under ten years of age in any regular work. I instruct them and give them exercise.'

His greatest success came when he set up a school. Owen would not allow **corporal punishment** to be used. For the very young children, he started the first infants' school in Britain.

Owen knew that other factory owners disliked him, because their workers wanted to be treated well. He tried to get Parliament to pass laws that would stop all children from working in factories.

Owen thought that people would be happier if they helped each other. In the USA, he tried to set up New Harmony, a village where everyone shared the work and the food equally. Sadly, quarrels broke out and his idea failed. But his son, also called Robert, became a US politician, supporting free schools for children, women's rights and an end to slavery.

For the rest of his life, Robert Owen supported **trade unions** and the **co-operative movement**. His ideas were very advanced for his time. He is more famous for what he tried to do than what he achieved, because many people did not share his views. Gradually, however, the employment of children was brought to an end.

Some people thought that Owen's ideas were silly. George Cruikshank drew this cartoon to poke fun at Owen's belief that everyone could live and work together happily in his village, New Harmony, in the USA.

DATE CHART

1771
Owen is born in Newtown, Wales.

1799
Marries Caroline Dale, daughter of the owner of the New Lanark spinning mill in Scotland.

1800
Begins the New Lanark 'experiment'.

1824–28
Tries to set up his New Harmony community in the USA.

1832–1858
Actively promotes the trade union and co-operative movement.

1858
17 November: dies in Newtown.

George Stephenson

1781 – 1848

'Masses of people lined the railroad, shouting and waving hats and handkerchiefs as we flew by them. I have never enjoyed anything so much as the first hour of our progress.'

This was how Fanny Kemble described her first train journey, on 15 September 1830, in a letter to a friend. However, at the start of the Industrial Revolution, goods and people could travel only as fast as their horses. Industry and business needed a quick, cheap way to transport their goods to every part of the country. The coming of the railways not only changed the appearance of the countryside, but also brought changes to everybody's way of life. The early success of the railways, and the idea of a rail network linking all the areas of Britain, were largely the work of George Stephenson.

George Stephenson built the world's first successful railways. They were one of the most important developments of the Industrial Revolution.

Like most people at that time, George had never been to school. He taught himself to read and started learning to be an engineer at a coal mine in north-east England. Soon he began to wonder whether there was an easier way of moving large amounts of coal than by horse-drawn wagons. He decided that he could improve on the work of Richard Trevithick, who had built a simple locomotive (railway engine).

Stephenson soon won a reputation for building successful locomotives and short railway lines to transport coal from the mines to local ports.

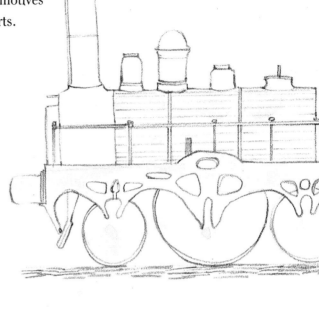

(above) This is a model of Richard Trevithick's early locomotive. He called it the 'Catch Me Who Can'. But his design was not strong enough to pull a proper train.

George and his son Robert designed many locomotives. This is an early design for the *Canterbury*.

Stephenson was asked to build a railway line to carry coal to Stockton and Darlington, in northern England. The line took three years to build, and when it opened, Stephenson drove the world's very first passenger train, pulled by the locomotive he had built, called *Locomotion*. Stephenson based the width between the rails, known as the gauge, on the width of horse-drawn wagons. This gauge of 143.5 cm is still the standard width of British railways.

OTHER IMPORTANT RAILWAY FIGURES

John Blenkinsop (1783–1831) – an early pioneer who built several successful locomotives.

George Hudson (1800–71) – the 'Railway King', who built and controlled thousands of kilometres of railways before losing everything when his business collapsed.

Isambard Brunel (1806–59) – an important engineer who built many things, including the Great Western Railway line and many ships, bridges and tunnels.

The *Rocket* locomotive was built to run on the Liverpool–Manchester Railway. It could reach a speed of 48 mph, which amazed people in 1830. It became the most famous railway locomotive ever built.

Stephenson's success led to him being employed to build a railway line linking the industrial city of Manchester to the important port of Liverpool. Many people warned that this would be too difficult, because some of the land was very marshy. Stephenson and his son, Robert, overcame all the obstacles in their way, and proved that a railway line could be built almost anywhere. Unfortunately, at the opening ceremony an important politician was hit by a train and injured. Stephenson took the controls of his *Rocket* locomotive and drove the politician several miles to a hospital near the line. Sadly the politician died, but the journey was faster than any ever made before, at 60 kph.

The Liverpool-Manchester railway line was an enormous success. People flocked to travel on it, and there was a sense of excitement and danger, as this early passenger described:

'The quickest motion to me is frightful; it is really flying . . . sparks of fire are abroad in some quantity; one burnt Miss de Ros's cheek, another a hole in Lady Maria's silk cloak . . .'

Some people opposed the railways. They thought that they were dangerous and would frighten farm animals. Unfortunately, on the early railways there were quite a few serious accidents.

Stephenson advised many of the companies which had been set up to build railways, and by the time he died it was possible to travel easily to and from any part of the country by train. As one passenger said about their first-ever train journey:

> *'Railway travelling is a delightful improvement of human life ... Everything is near, everything is immediate – time, distance and delay are abolished.'*

For his achievements, George Stephenson is often called 'the father of the railways'.

(below and opposite) Trains on the Liverpool–Manchester railway line in the 1830s. On the left are goods wagons. In the picture on the right, you can see first and second-class passenger carriages. For the very first time, people could travel long distances quickly and cheaply.

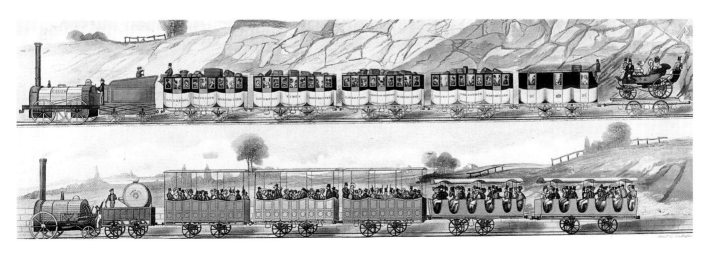

Louis Daguerre

1787 – 1851

'From today, painting is dead!'

This was exclaimed by an anonymous French artist after he had seen Louis Daguerre's invention – the first practical camera. Daguerre was a famous painter in his home country, France, for a long time before he started taking photographs.

At the age of thirteen, he drew portraits of his parents that convinced them of his great talent, and he was apprenticed to a local architect. But Daguerre was not particularly interested in designing buildings; he wanted to paint landscape pictures and people's portraits.

This early form of camera, called a camera obscura, belonged to the British King George III.

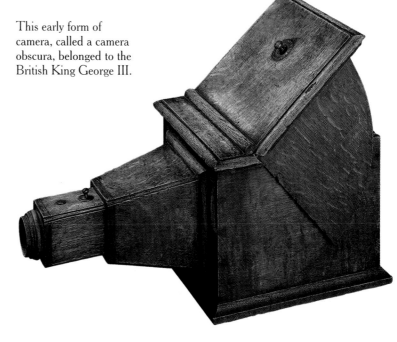

After a great deal of family argument, Daguerre persuaded his father to let him go to Paris to study art. In Paris he lived as a lodger at the home of a well-known stage designer. He helped to design and paint scenery at the **Opéra** and other theatres, and painted huge pictures of mountain ranges and landscapes, known as panoramas. But it was his *Diorama* that made Daguerre famous across the country. He set up an exhibition of large, transparent paintings, and used all kinds of different lighting and even sound effects to make them appear real.

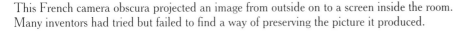
This French camera obscura projected an image from outside on to a screen inside the room. Many inventors had tried but failed to find a way of preserving the picture it produced.

Daguerre then began to think of a way that people might make realistic pictures for themselves. He knew about the **camera obscura**, where light enters a box through a pin-hole and produces a picture of what is outside the box, and he wanted to find a way of preserving the picture. He teamed up with another French inventor, Joseph Niepce, who took the first-ever photograph. It was very simple, but it was a step forward. Four years later, Niepce died and Daguerre worked on alone.

OTHER EARLY PHOTOGRAPHERS

Joseph Niepce (1765–1833) – a colleague of Daguerre who took the first-ever photograph.

William Fox Talbot (1800–77) – invented the first method of printing photographs from negatives.

Mathew Brady (1823–96) – a pioneer photographer who became famous for his many photographs of the US Civil War.

Julia Margaret Cameron (1815–79) – famous for her artistic, life-like pictures.

33

This is the first-ever photograph. It was taken by Joseph Niepce in 1826 from the attic window of his house, and shows his courtyard. It took eight hours to take this photograph.

Daguerre experimented with metal plates covered with various chemicals. Louise, his wife, worried that he had set himself an impossible task and thought he might go mad. Jean Dumas, an important scientist, reassured her:

'At present it cannot be done; but I cannot say it will always remain impossible, nor set down as mad who seeks to do it.'

It took Louis ten years to discover that if he coated a plate with a chemical called silver iodide he could produce a satisfactory picture, or photograph.

There was great excitement when Louis announced his invention, which he called the Daguerreotype. Using his camera, Louis said:

'Everyone will make a view of his castle or country-house.'

This shows that Louis hoped to sell his invention to wealthy people! Soon, many photographers had set up in business producing Daguerreotypes. Samuel Morse, an American painter and inventor, said that the machine was

'... one of the most beautiful discoveries of the age.

34

Thousands of photographic studios were set up all over the world. As a result of Daguerre's invention we are able to see photographs of people and places exactly as they were in the 1840s.

'The Chess Players' is an early framed Daguerreotype. This chess game was played more than 150 years ago.

Many studios were set up to take Daguerreotype portraits like this one. They became very popular. For the first time, people could have real pictures of their friends or family to keep with them.

However, one problem with the Daguerreotype was that only one print could be made of each picture. A year later, William Fox Talbot, from Britain, announced a different process that could produce any number of prints from the same **negative**. In the end, this method proved to be better than Daguerre's, but it was Daguerre who first showed the world the possibilities of photography.

DATE CHART

1787
Daguerre is born in Corneille, France.

1807–22
Works as a painter and set designer in Paris.

1810
Marries Louise Smith, who has English parents but grew up in France.

1822
Opens the *Diorama* in Paris (and later one in London).

1824
Begins to experiment with photography.

1829
Teams up with Joseph Niepce, who has taken the very first photograph.

1833
Niepce dies.

1839
Daguerre announces the invention of the daguerreotype camera. His process of photography becomes widely popular, and many thousands of portrait studios are set up throughout the world.

1851
Daguerre dies.

35

Elizabeth Gaskell

1810 – 65

'Whole streets, unpaved and without drains or main sewers, are worn into deep ruts and holes in which water constantly stagnates, and are so covered with refuse and other filth that it is almost impossible to use them because of the deep mud and dreadful smell.'

That was how a doctor described the streets of Manchester, England during the Industrial Revolution. Thousands of people lived and worked in overcrowded and unhealthy **slums**. Lack of clean water helped spread the terrible diseases cholera and typhoid.

Elizabeth Gaskell was a successful writer who described to her well-off readers how poor people lived in the industrial cities.

36

Manchester had grown very rapidly. Because it was the centre of the cotton industry it was sometimes known as 'Cottonopolis'. Wealthy people were not interested in the conditions of the working classes, and did not want their tax money to be spent on improvements. But there were some **reformers** who were very worried.

MANCHESTER, FROM KERSALL MOOR.—(SEE NEXT PAGE.)

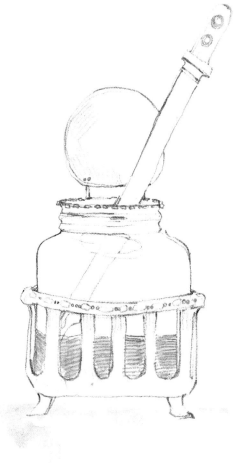

(above) Manchester, England, grew very quickly during the Industrial Revolution into a large and important factory city. But the streets were unpaved and there was no proper water supply or rubbish collection.

(below) Huge cotton mills like this one made Manchester the capital of the cotton industry. Men, women and children worked long hours without any holidays in these factories. At night, they went home to filthy, over-crowded slum houses.

37

An entire family would live in a room like this one, with no furniture. They would have to share an outside toilet with other families. Elizabeth Gaskell wrote about these dreadful conditions in her books.

Elizabeth Gaskell used her talent as a writer to tell her readers about the conditions in the industrial cities. As a child, she had a comfortable and pleasant life, and knew very little about the problems faced by the **working classes** in the cities. However, her life changed dramatically after she married a religious minister, William Gaskell. It was a great shock to her when she saw the harsh life of his **parishioners** in Manchester. Entire families lived in a single room without a toilet or running water, while thousands of people lived in cellars which were frequently flooded with muck from the unmade roads. Wages were low, and at times of high unemployment many families were constantly hungry. The *Manchester Times* newspaper described people in the city:

'... hungry and half-clothed men and women are stalking through the streets begging for bread.'

In her own life, Gaskell suffered tragedy. Her brother, a sailor, was drowned at sea. Her first child was born dead, and later her baby son William died. Gaskell eventually discovered that she had the talent to write books. Out of her own personal sorrow, as well as her disgust at the poverty she saw in Manchester, she wrote a novel called *Mary Barton*.

When it was published a **critic** wrote:

'Do the rich want to know why poor men learn to hate law and order, in other words to hate the rich? Then let them read Mary Barton'

38

The book was extremely popular, but it shocked many people with its descriptions of the poor, such as this one:

'The cellar in which a family of human beings lived was very dark inside. Three or four children were rolling on the damp, nay wet, brick floor, through which the stagnant, filthy moisture of the street oozed up; the fire-place was empty and black.'

Like Gaskell before her marriage, most of her readers had no idea that poor people led such miserable lives. Gaskell opened their eyes to how most people lived. She became a highly respected author, but in spite of her success she remained busy as a minister's wife, helping unemployed mill-workers who could not afford to buy food for their families. Throughout her adult life, Gaskell was concerned simply with the kindness of human beings towards each other. At the age of fifty-five, she died quite suddenly while having her afternoon tea – her tireless and difficult work had exhausted her.

Some wealthy women liked to visit and help the sick and poor. But charity was not enough. Very slowly, the government began to take action to improve living conditions in the towns.

OTHER POPULAR WRITERS

Jane Austen (1775–1817) – author of six novels which are still popular today.

William Thackeray (1811–63) – author of *Vanity Fair*.

Charles Dickens (1812–70) – author of many famous novels, such as *Oliver Twist*, which describe life in Victorian Britain in great detail.

Charlotte Brontë (1816–55) – author of several novels, including *Jane Eyre*.

George Eliot (1819–80) – her real name was Mary Evans, and in her books she challenged many established Victorian ideas.

Harriet Tubman

1820/21 – 1913

I looked at my hands to see if I was the same person now I was free. There was such a glory over everything, the sun comes like gold through the trees.

This first experience of freedom felt very good for a brave **African American**, Harriet Tubman, after she had escaped from slavery. The terrible system of keeping black slaves was legal in the southern states of the USA. The slaves worked long hours for no wages in **plantations** which produced raw cotton. A great deal of the cotton was exported to British cotton mills in Lancashire. This cheap cotton made factory owners a great deal of profit during the Industrial Revolution.

At slave auctions like this one in 1861, human beings were bought and sold as if they were animals. Often families were split up and sold to different people.

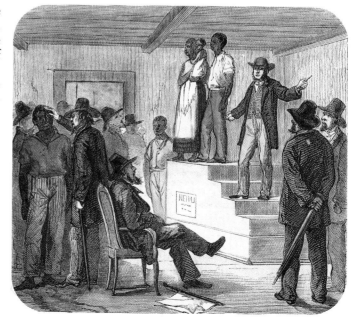

Tubman was born into slavery. She was one of the eleven children of Harriet and Benjamin Ross, but she was the property of a white slave-owner. As a child and a teenager she worked in the fields under terrible conditions. Her owner said she was '*stupid*' and '*not worth six cents*'. When she was fifteen, her head was injured when she was hit by a brutal **overseer**. As a slave she had no right to protection, or even to choose the man that she married. Her master forced her to marry another slave called Tubman. But from an early age, she knew that slavery was evil, and she was determined to fight against it.

Sometimes slaves were brutally whipped. However, these and other terrible punishments did not stop the slaves from rebelling and trying to escape.

When she was about twenty-five, Tubman took a great risk and escaped. She made her way along the 'Underground Railroad', as it was known, to the north where she would be free. This was not a real underground railway, but a secret route along which slaves were hidden and helped by white people opposed to slavery as they made their escape. If the fleeing slaves were caught, they would be severely beaten or even killed. Tubman, however was not afraid of death:

'There was one of two things
I had a right to, liberty or death;
if I could not have one, I would
have the other; for no man
should take me alive.'

$50 Reward.

RANAWAY from the Subscriber, living in the county of Edgecombe, N. C. about eight miles north of Tarborough, on the 24th of August last, **a** negro fellow named WASHINGTON, about 24 years of age, 5 feet 8 or 10 inches high, dark complexion, stout built, and an excellent field hand—no particular marks about him recollected. The said fellow was formerly owned by Mr. Jas. Taylor, of Martin county, and I think it more than probable that he is now lurking in the neighborhood of Taylor's Ferry. The above reward of *Fifty Dollars*, will be given to any person who will apprehend said negro and deliver him to me, or lodge him in jail so that I get him again. All persons are hereby forbid harboring or employing said fellow under penalty of the law.

JOHN LAWRENCE.

Oct. 4, 1827.

DATE CHART

1820 or 1821
Tubman is born into slavery in Bucktown, Maryland, USA.

1849
She escapes to freedom in the north.

1850–61
Makes many trips back to the south to help other slaves to escape.

1861–65
During the Civil War, she serves as a nurse, laundress and spy for the Union Army. The war brings slavery to an end.

1866–1913
Sets up schools for people who have been slaves. Supports many humanitarian causes. Opens a home for aged African Americans.

1913
10 March: dies at Auburn, New York.

Once she had reached the north she could have stayed there in safety, but she was determined to help others and to do all she could to destroy slavery. As a strong Christian, she believed that God was guiding her work. Time and again she risked her life to return and help other slaves escape. She became the most famous 'conductor' on the 'railroad'. In the end she rescued more than 300 slaves. White southerners hated her and offered a reward of $40,000 for her capture. Harriet always carried a gun and warned the fleeing slaves, 'You'll be free or die'. A white **abolitionist** called her:

'... one of the best and bravest persons on this continent – General Tubman as we call her'.

It took four years of terrible **civil war** to finally end slavery, and Tubman did all she could to help defeat the South. After it was all over, she took up many other good causes, and lived into her nineties. To African Americans she is known as the **'Moses** of her people' because, like Moses in the story, she led so many slaves into freedom.

Many American cities were ruined by the terrible civil war that was fought to end slavery. By the end of the war, 620,000 American soldiers had died. Slavery had tragic results for all Americans.

(below) Former slaves, celebrating their freedom. They travelled North to start a new life. Sadly, however, racial discrimination against black people in the USA continued to be a problem.

OTHER SLAVES WHO FOUGHT FOR FREEDOM

Sojourner Truth (1797–1883)
– a runaway slave who spent more than forty years preaching and arguing against slavery.

Nat Turner (1800–31)
– he organized a rebellion by more than 60 slaves, but was captured and hanged.

Frederick Douglass (1817–95)
– the most important leader of black Americans during the US Civil War.

Glossary

Abolitionist Someone who wanted to stop the system of slavery.

African American A black American who is descended from the people taken from Africa to America as slaves.

Apprentice Someone who works with another person, to learn that person's trade.

British Empire Countries controlled by Britain. The Empire came to an end during the first half of the twentieth century.

Camera obscura Means 'a darkened room'. Light passes through a small hole or lens and makes a picture on the opposite side or wall.

Civil War A war between different groups of people who live in the same country.

Colossus A huge or impressive person.

Co-operative movement Where people work and trade together, with each person taking a fair share of the profits.

Corporal punishment Punishment by beating or caning.

Critic A critic writes or speaks about something, pointing out its good and bad points.

Domestic system Goods such as cloth being made in people's own homes. This was the way things were made before the factory system.

Feminist Someone who supports equal rights for women.

French Revolution A violent uprising in 1789 which ended the power of the royal family and set up the French Republic (1792).

Humanitarian A person who works to reduce other people's suffering.

Moses In the thirteenth century BC, Moses led the Jewish people out of Egypt into freedom.

Negative The picture on a photographic film when the areas of light and dark are reversed. Prints are made from a negative.

Opéra The Opéra in Paris is the famous theatre where performances of operas (plays in which the words are sung to music), take place.

Overseer Somebody who supervises other people.

Parishioner Someone living in an area with its own church and priest.

Plantation A large area of land where crops are grown.

Prophecy A statement telling people what will happen in the future.

Protestants Christians who belong to a church that is not part of the Roman Catholic Church, such as the Church of England.

Rebellion When people fight against a ruler or government.

Reformers People who try to improve laws and living conditions.

Roman Catholics Christians who belong to the Roman Catholic Church. They believe that their leader, the Pope, is God's messenger.

Slums Very poor-quality houses which are overcrowded, dirty, and often do not have toilets or a proper supply of water.

Suspension bridge A bridge that is suspended or hung from cables stretching from each side and does not have any pillars holding it up.

Trade union A group of workers of the same trade who join together to bargain with employers for changes such as higher wages.

Working classes The people who worked in manual jobs such as in factories and coal mines, and building ships, roads and railways.

44

Books to read

John D. Clare, *I Was There – Industrial Revolution* (Bodley Head, 1993)
Henry Dale, *Early Flying Machines* (The British Library, 1992)
A. Feldman and P. Ford, *Scientists and Inventors* (Bloomsbury Books, 1989)
Douglas McTavish, *Famous Inventors* (Wayland, 1993)

Nigel Hunter, *Twenty Campaigners for Change* (Wayland, 1987)
Nigel Smith, *Black Peoples of the Americas* (Oxford University Press, 1992)
Nigel Smith, *The Industrial Revolution* (Wayland, 1990)
Annabel Wigner, *Timeline Ireland* (Dryad Press, 1988)

Places to visit

James Watt
The Science Museum, Exhibition Road, London SW7, England. Tel: 0171 938 8000.
Birmingham Museum of Science & Industry, Newhall Street, Birmingham, England. Tel: 0121 235 1661.
McClean Museum, West End, Greenock, Renfrewshire, Scotland. Tel: 01475 723741.
The Steam Museum, Straffan, Co Kildare, Dublin, Ireland. Tel: (1) 627 3155.
The Royal Museum of Scotland, Chambers Street, Edinburgh, Scotland. Tel: 0131 225 7534.

Joseph Montgolfier
Monument on Avenue Marc-Seguin, Annonay, Rhône Valley, France.

Thomas Telford
Waterloo Bridge at Betws-y-Coed, Wales.
The Menai Straits Bridge, Wales.

Mary Wollstonecraft
Mary Wollstonecraft is buried in St Peter's Churchyard, Bournemouth, Dorset, England.

William Wilberforce
Wilberforce House Museum, 25 High Street, Hull, England. Tel: 01482 593902.
William Wilberforce statue in Queen's Gardens, Hull, England.

Wolfe Tone
Wolfe Tone's grave at Bodentown Churchyard, near Naas, Co Kildare, Ireland.
1796 French Armada Exhibition Centre, Bantry House, Bantry, Co Cork, Ireland.

Robert Owen
New Lanark Village, Lanark, Scotland. Tel: 01555 61345.
Robert Owen Memorial Museum, The Cross, Broad Street, Newtown, Powys, Wales. Tel: 01686 625544.
Historic New Harmony, Indiana, USA. Tel: 812 682 4488.

George Stephenson
Museum of Science & Industry, Castlefield, Manchester, England. Tel: 0161 832 2244.
National Railway Museum, Leeman Road, York, England. Tel: 01904 621261.
Darlington Railway Centre & Museum, North Road Station, Darlington, Co Durham, England. Tel: 01325 460532.

Louis Daguerre
Fox Talbot Museum, Lacock, Wiltshire, England. Tel: 01249 730459.
International Museum of Photography, George Eastman House, Rochester, New York, USA. Tel: 712 271 3361.

Elizabeth Gaskell
Elizabeth Gaskell is buried at the Unitarian Chapel, Adam's Hill, Knutsford, Cheshire, England.

Harriet Tubman
Anacostia Museum of African American History, 1901 Fort Place, Washington DC, USA. Tel: 202 357 2700.
Harriet Tubman's Home, 180 South Street, Auburn, New York. Tel: 315 252 2081.

I n d e x